Ketogenic Diet

Recipes

Healthy, Low-Carb Recipes Ideas Just for Two

Magda Williams

no scenarios in which the publisher or the original author of this work can be in any fashion deemed liable for any hardship or damages that may befall them after undertaking information described herein.

Additionally, the information in the following pages is intended only for informational purposes and should thus be thought of as universal. As befitting its nature, it is presented without assurance regarding its prolonged validity or interim quality. Trademarks that are mentioned are done without written consent and can in no way be considered an endorsement from the trademark holder.

TABLE OF CONTENTS

Introduction

The Ketogenic Diet works by drastically reducing carbohydrates in the diet. When this happens, the liver converts fat into ketone bodies, used for energy by every cell in your body. The body then makes use of these ketones, often referred to as "ketones" and "ketone bodies," through a process called "beta-oxidation" to produce energy (ATP) that is not reliant on insulin.

Ketosis is a natural physiological state of your body. When your body is in ketosis, it begins burning fat for producing energy rather than using sugar.

People adopt a ketogenic diet for different reasons, to lose weight and belly fat or to reduce their risk of having certain illnesses like diabetes, etc.

The Keto Diet remains one of the most popular throughout the world. Studies have shown that the ketogenic diet is far more effective than a low-fat diet at maintaining weight loss in the long term.

Aside from incredible weight loss results, Keto dieters have also reported:

>Increased energy levels

>Improved acne and skin health

>Regulated blood sugar levels

>Lowered 'bad' cholesterol and improved healthy cholesterol

>Stronger focus and mental clarity

>Staying full for longer and reduced cravings

>Decreased blood pressure in overweight individuals

>Better control over epileptic symptoms in both children and adults.

This Ketogenic Diet for Two Recipes is perfectly suited for two people.

Ketogenic Recipes

Keto Omelet Caprese with Cheese

Time required:
15 minutes

Servings: 02

INGREDIENTS	STEPS FOR COOKING
6 eggs Salt and pepper 1 tablespoon fresh basil, chopped or dried 2 tablespoons olive oil 75g cherry tomatoes, cut in half or slices 150 g fresh mozzarella cheese, diced or sliced	1. Break eggs into a large bowl, then season with salt and pepper. 2. Beat the eggs well with a fork. Add the basil and mix everything thoroughly. 3. Heat oil in a large skillet. Roast the tomatoes for a few minutes. 4. Pour the beaten eggs over the tomatoes. Wait for the omelet to harden a little and then add the mozzarella.

Morning Hash

Time required:
40 minutes

Servings: 02

INGREDIENTS

½ teaspoon dried thyme, crushed

½ small onion, chopped

1 tablespoon butter

½ cup cauliflower florets, boiled

¼ cup heavy cream

Salt and black pepper, to taste

½ pound cooked turkey meat, chopped

STEPS FOR COOKING

1. Finely chop cauliflowers. Sauté butter and onion, then add chopped cauliflower.
2. Put turkey and let it cook. Mix in heavy cream and keep mixing it.
3. Serve.

Avocado Bun Breakfast Burger

Time required:
15 minutes

Servings: 02

INGREDIENTS

1 avocado

1 egg

1 oz breakfast sausage

1 tbsp sesame seeds

1 tbsp mayonnaise

1 pinch salt and pepper 1 sliced tomato

1 tbsp olive oil

1 lettuce leaf

STEPS FOR COOKING

1. Place the avocado horizontally on its side and slice it right in the middle. Remove the seed and spoon out the flesh carefully.

2. Heat the oil in a skillet. Cook breakfast sausage over medium-low heat for 1-2 min on each side until well toasted.

3. In the skillet, crack the egg open, turn the heat down, cover, and cook with the sunny side up. Be sure the egg white is cooked.

4. Place the lower half of the avocado on a plate, spoon some mayo into the avocado hole and top with lettuce, tomato, sausage. Add the egg carefully and top with the other half of the avocado.

5. Sprinkle salt, pepper, and sesame seeds as desired.

Cheddar Spinach Omelet

Time required:
17 minutes

Servings: 02

INGREDIENTS	STEPS FOR COOKING
4 large eggs 1½ cups chopped fresh spinach leaves 2 tablespoons peeled and chopped yellow onion 2 tablespoons salted butter, melted ½ cup shredded mild Cheddar cheese ¼ teaspoon salt	1. In an ungreased 6-inch round nonstick baking dish, whisk eggs. Stir in spinach, onion, butter, Cheddar, and salt. 2. Place dish into air fryer basket. Adjust the temperature to 320°F (160ºC) and set the timer for 12 minutes. Omelet will be done when browned on the top and firm in the middle. 3. Slice in half and serve warm on two medium plates.

Almond Flour Waffles

Time required:
30 minutes

Servings: 02

INGREDIENTS

*100g blanched
almond flour*

60ml heavy cream

2 eggs

1 tsp vanilla extract

2 tbsp erythritol

2 tbsp coconut oil

2 tbsp butter

1 tsp baking powder

STEPS FOR COOKING

1. Preheat your waffle maker and lightly grease with coconut oil.

2. In a bowl, beat the eggs and whisk with vanilla extract, heavy cream, and erythritol.

3. Slowly incorporate almond flour and baking powder into the mixture.

4. Add a pinch of salt and stir until completely smooth.

5. Spoon the waffle batter into the preheated waffle maker.

6. Cook for about 5 minutes or until the waffles are golden.

7. Continue with the rest of the waffle batter until finished.

8. Serve with a tablespoon of butter for every two waffles.

Breakfast Crepes

Time required:
27 minutes

Servings: 02

INGREDIENTS

2 eggs, beaten

2 ounces cream cheese, softened

1 tablespoon butter

The ground cinnamon, to taste

Any sugar-free syrup to taste (optional)

STEPS FOR COOKING

1. Pick a mixing bowl and add eggs with the cream cheese.
2. Blend it into a smooth mixture.
3. Add syrup and cinnamon to taste.
4. Heat butter in a pan and add in the mixed batter.
5. Cook on medium fire and leave on heat for a couple of minutes on each side.
6. Turn carefully with a spatula and shift to plate when it becomes brown.
7. Serve.

Keto Oatmeal

Time required:
30 minutes

Servings: 02

INGREDIENTS	STEPS FOR COOKING

2 tablespoons flaxseeds

2 tablespoons sunflower seeds

2 cups coconut milk

2 tablespoons chia seeds

2 pinches of salt

1. Mix all ingredients in a saucepan, then let it simmer.
2. Dish out in a bowl and serve warm.

No Bread Keto Breakfast Sandwich

Time required:
15 minutes

Servings: 02

INGREDIENTS	STEPS FOR COOKING

INGREDIENTS

2 tbsp butter

4 eggs

1 oz smoked deli ham

2 oz cheddar or Provolone cheese, cut in thick slices

Salt and pepper

Tabasco sauce

STEPS FOR COOKING

1. Heat butter frying pan over medium heat. Fry the eggs on both sides and add salt and pepper.
2. For each "sandwich," use a fried egg as the base, then place the ham on top, then add the cheese. Use a fried egg to top off each stack. Leave the cheese to melt over low heat if desired.
3. Serve immediately with a few drops of Tabasco sauce.

Mozzarella Bacon Pizza

Time required:
15 minutes

Servings: 02

INGREDIENTS

1 cup shredded
Mozzarella cheese

1 ounce (28 g)
cream cheese,
broken into small
pieces

4 slices cooked
sugar-free bacon,
chopped

¼ cup chopped
pickled jalapeños

1 large egg, whisked

¼ teaspoon salt

STEPS FOR COOKING

1. Place Mozzarella in a single layer on
    the bottom of an ungreased 6- inch
    round nonstick baking dish. Scatter
    cream cheese pieces, bacon, and
    jalapeños over Mozzarella, then pour
    egg evenly around the baking dish.

2. Sprinkle with salt and place into an air
    fryer basket. Adjust the temperature
    to 330°F (166ºC) and set the timer for
    10 minutes. When cheese is brown
    and egg is set, pizza will be done.

3. Let cool on a large plate 5 minutes
    before serving.

Keto Croque Madame

Time required:
5 minutes

Servings: 02

INGREDIENTS	STEPS FOR COOKING

INGREDIENTS

1 medium zucchini

1 tablespoon grated red onion

2 extra-large eggs lightly beaten

3 tablespoons all-purpose flour

½ tablespoons ground black pepper

½ tablespoon salt

vegetable oil

1 teaspoon of baking powder

STEPS FOR COOKING

1. Preheat the oven to over 300 degrees Fahrenheit.

2. In a mixing bowl, grate the zucchini and add the onions and eggs right away.

3. Combine the flour, baking powder, salt, and pepper in a mixing bowl.

4. Add the vegetable oil to a big sauté pan and steam over medium heat.

5. Reduce the heat to medium-low and pour the batter into the pan once the oil is hot. Cook both sides for about 2 minutes.

Yummy Muffin

Time required:
40 minutes

Servings: 02

INGREDIENTS

1 egg

*1 slice bacon,
chopped and cooked*

*2 tablespoons
almond flour*

*¼ cup veggies salsa
or leftovers*

*Oil for greasing the
baking pan*

STEPS FOR COOKING

1. Prepare a baking dish at 350F.
2. Grease 2 cups for muffins.
3. Blend the salsa with bacon, almond flour, and egg.
4. Divide this blended mixture into the cups evenly.
5. Bake for 30 minutes till done, use a toothpick to check the completion.
6. Leave for 10 minutes and then serve.

Blueberry Smoothie

Time required:
5 minutes

Servings: 02

INGREDIENTS	STEPS FOR COOKING
1 cup fresh blueberries	1. Blend all ingredients until smooth, then pour it into the glasses.
1 teaspoon vanilla extract	2. Serve and enjoy.
28 ounces coconut milk	
2 tablespoons lemon juice	

Cinnamon Chaffee

Time required:
6 minutes

Servings: 02

INGREDIENTS

1 egg
½ cup mozzarella
½ tsp cinnamon
½ tsp vanilla

STEPS FOR COOKING

1. Heat waffle maker.
2. Whisk egg.
3. Add cheese and other ingredients then cook for4 minutes.
4. Remove and cool 2-3 minutes.

Bacon Quiche with Cheddar Cheese

Time required:
17 minutes

Servings: 02

INGREDIENTS	STEPS FOR COOKING

3 large eggs

2 tablespoons heavy whipping cream

¼ teaspoon salt

4 slices cooked sugar-free bacon, crumbled

½ cup shredded mild Cheddar cheese

1. In a large bowl, whisk eggs, cream, and salt together until combined, then mix in bacon and Cheddar.

2. Pour mixture evenly into two ungreased 4-inch ramekins. Place into air fryer basket. Adjust the temperature to 320°F (160ºC) and set the timer for 12 minutes. Quiche will be fluffy and set in the middle when done.

3. Let quiche cool in ramekins 5 minutes. Serve warm.

One-Pan Garlic Chicken and Broccoli

Time required:
35 minutes

Servings: 02

INGREDIENTS

200g broccoli florets

120g boneless chicken thighs

150g cherry tomatoes

60g cream cheese

5 garlic cloves

2 tbsps extra virgin olive oil

½ tsp of Italian seasoning

STEPS FOR COOKING

1. Mince the garlic and halve the cherry tomatoes.

2. Heat the olive oil in a large skillet or pan at medium-high heat. Add the chicken thighs. Season with salt and pepper. Cook until golden for about 4-5 minutes on each side.

3. Add minced garlic to the pan and cook with the chicken thighs for 1 minute.

4. Add broccoli, tomatoes, and cream cheese to the pan. Cook with Italian seasoning for 4 minutes or until broccoli is tender and cooked through.

5. Serve and enjoy.

Mushroom Flank Steaks

Time required:
2 hours 30
minutes

Servings: 02

INGREDIENTS	STEPS FOR COOKING

INGREDIENTS

3 tbsp. extra-virgin olive oil

1 lb. beef flank steaks

1 c. button mushrooms

1 t. of each:

Finely chopped fresh rosemary

Salt

2 t. blue cheese

STEPS FOR COOKING

1. Rinse the steaks and rub them with oil. Give them a sprinkle of rosemary and salt. Arrange each one in a Ziploc bag, remove the air, and seal.

2. Set the timer for 2 hours at 154ºF. When done, remove from the water cooker and set to the side.

3. Warm up one tablespoon of the oil to a hot skillet and melt the blue cheese. Toss in the mushrooms and steak. Sear for about 5 minutes until the mushrooms are softened and the steaks have browned to your liking.

Buffalo Chicken Soup with Celery

Time required:
17 minutes

Servings: 02

INGREDIENTS	STEPS FOR COOKING
1 ounce (28 g) celery stalk, chopped 4 tablespoons coconut milk ¾ teaspoon salt ¼ teaspoon white pepper 1 cup water 2 ounces (57 g) Mozzarella, shredded 6 ounces (170 g) cooked chicken, shredded 2 tablespoons keto-friendly Buffalo sauce	1. Place the chopped celery stalk, coconut milk, salt, white pepper, water, and Mozzarella in the Instant Pot. Stir to mix well. 2. Set the Manual mode and set the timer for 7 minutes on High Pressure. 3. When the timer beeps, use a quick pressure release and open the lid. 4. Transfer the soup to the bowls. Stir in the chicken and Buffalo sauce. Serve warm.

Caprese Stuffed Mushrooms

Time required:
35 minutes

Servings: 02

INGREDIENTS

4 portobello mushrooms

3 garlic clove

120g baby tomatoes

2 tbsps extra virgin olive oil

4 mozzarella balls

2 tsp fresh or dried basil

½ tsp balsamic vinegar

STEPS FOR COOKING

1. Preheat the oven to 200°C.
2. Chop the baby tomatoes in half and dice the garlic. Pat-dry the mozzarella balls and thinly slice them.
3. Twist off stems from the mushrooms and scoop out the gills from under the mushroom cap.
4. In a small bowl, coat the mushrooms in olive oil and salt to taste.
5. Bake mushrooms for 9-10 minutes or until mushrooms have softened.
6. In the same oiled bowl, combine the mozzarella cheese, chopped tomatoes, diced garlic, and half of the basil. Season with salt and pepper. Mix well.

INGREDIENTS	STEPS FOR COOKING

7. Remove the portobello mushrooms from the oven. Fill with the Caprese mixture.

8. Bake stuffed mushrooms for 11-14 minutes or until tomatoes have softened.

9. Add a dash of balsamic vinegar to each mushroom.

10. Top with any remaining basil and serve.

Beef and Vegetable Skillet

Time required:
20 minutes

Servings: 02

INGREDIENTS	STEPS FOR COOKING
3 oz spinach, chopped	1. Take a skillet pan, place it over medium heat, add oil and when hot, add beef and bacon and cook for 5 to 7 minutes until slightly browned.
½ pound ground beef	
2 slices of bacon, diced	2. Then add asparagus and spinach, sprinkle with thyme, stir well and cook for 7 to 10 minutes until thoroughly cooked.
2 oz chopped asparagus	
Seasoning:	3. Season skillet with salt and black pepper and serve.
3 tbsp coconut oil	
2 tsp dried thyme	
2/3 tsp salt	
½ tsp ground black pepper	

Pita Pizza

Time required:
25 minutes

Servings: 02

INGREDIENTS

½ cup Marinara
sauce
1 low-carb pita
2 oz. Cheddar
cheese
14 Pepperoni slices
1 oz. Roasted red
peppers

STEPS FOR COOKING

1. Set oven to 450º Fahrenheit.
2. Slice the pita in half and place it onto a foil-lined baking tray. Rub with a bit of oil and toast for 2 minutes.
3. Pour the sauce over the bread. Sprinkle using the cheese and other toppings. Bake for 5 minutes.

Kale, Lemon, and White Bean Soup

Time required:
1 hour 10
minutes

Servings: 02

INGREDIENTS	STEPS FOR COOKING

INGREDIENTS

150 grams of dried cannellini beans

2 cups of vegetable stock

5 cups of water

1 white onion, diced

2 tbsps. of olive oil

8 cloves of garlic

Kombu (one-inch strip)

1 tsp. of dried thyme

2 small potatoes, cubed after peeling

2 bay leaves

1 cup of kale

1 lemon, juiced, and zest

STEPS FOR COOKING

1. Take an ample amount of water to soak the dried beans and keep them soaked for about twelve hours. Drain the beans properly and they should become double their size, then rinse them.

2. Take a large-sized pot, and in it, add one tbsp. of oil and heat it. Then, add the diced onion to the pot and cook the onions until they become golden and soft.

3. Then, add the stock and water along with garlic, dried beans, kombu, thyme, and bay leaves. Keep the pot covered and then bring it to a boil. Once it starts boiling, reduce the flame to a simmer and wait for about forty minutes.

INGREDIENTS	STEPS FOR COOKING

4. While it is cooking, start with the kale. Wash it thoroughly. All the inner stalks that are tough should be removed. Then, start slicing them into ribbons of one inch each. It looks good when you have delicate small pieces, so you should take your time with this.

5. After about half an hour, add the potatoes to the pot and then let the preparation simmer for ten more minutes. After this, both the potatoes and the beans should be soft. Take out the kombu and bay leaves. Take a potato masher and use it carefully to mash at least half of the beans and potatoes.

6. Add the kale. Cook the mixture for ten more minutes. The water content needs to be checked now and see whether it is right or whether it needs to be topped up a bit. If the water is too much, then cook uncovered for a few minutes so that it dries up.

7. Once you notice the kale softening, take a tbsp. of olive oil and add it to the pot. Stir in the zest and lemon juice as well, and your dish is ready.

Chicken Zoodles Soup

Time required:
40 minutes

Servings: 02

INGREDIENTS

2 cups water

*6 ounces (170 g)
chicken fillet,
chopped*

1 teaspoon salt

*2 ounces (57 g)
zucchini, spiralized*

*1 tablespoon
coconut aminos*

STEPS FOR COOKING

1. Pour water into the Instant Pot. Add chopped chicken fillet and salt. Close the lid.

2. Select Manual mode and set the cooking time for 15 minutes on High Pressure.

3. When cooking is complete, perform a natural pressure release for 10 minutes, then release any remaining pressure. Open the lid.

4. Fold in the zoodles and coconut aminos.

5. Leave the soup for 10 minutes to rest. Serve warm.

Watermelon and Prosciutto Salad

Time required:
15 minutes

Servings: 02

INGREDIENTS

280g rocket or spinach

180g diced watermelon

120g crumbled feta cheese

8 slices of prosciutto

2 red onions

3 tbsps extra virgin olive oil

2 tbsp balsamic or white vinegar

1 tbsp mustard

1 tsp salt

1 bunch fresh mint (optional)

STEPS FOR COOKING

1. Dice the red onions, then set them aside while you make the dressing.

2. In a bowl, combine the olive oil, vinegar, mustard, and salt, then Stir or whisk together.

3. Add the rocket, shredded prosciutto, and onions to the bowl. Toss until the leaves are fully coated in dressing.

4. Once mixed, add the diced tomato and crumbled feta cheese on top. Lightly toss, but not too much or the salad will get soggy.

5. Serve with fresh mint leaves and enjoy.

Cheesy Meatloaf

Time required:
10 minutes

Servings: 02

INGREDIENTS	STEPS FOR COOKING
4 oz ground turkey *1 egg* *1 tbsp grated mozzarella cheese* *¼ tsp Italian seasoning* *½ tbsp soy sauce* *Seasoning:* *¼ tsp salt* *1/8 tsp ground black pepper*	1. Take a bowl, place all the ingredients in it, and stir until mixed. 2. Take a heatproof mug, spoon in the prepared mixture, and microwave for 3 minutes at a high heat setting until cooked. 3. When done, let meatloaf rest in the mug for 1 minute, then take it out, cut it into two slices and serve.

Bacon-Wrapped Turkey Breast

Time required:
1 hour 10
minutes

Servings: 02

INGREDIENTS

¾ pound turkey
breast

½ teaspoons dried
rosemary

½ teaspoons dried
thyme

½ teaspoons dried
sage

6 large bacon slices

STEPS FOR COOKING

1. Preheat the oven to 350ºF. Ready baking sheet with parchment paper. Sprinkle with herbs.

2. Wrap the bacon slices around the turkey breast.

3. Place onto the prepared baking sheet and cover with foil, and bake for 50 minutes.

4. Remove the foil, then bake for 10 minutes.

5. Pull out baking sheet from oven and set aside for 10 minutes.

6. Cut the turkey breast and serve.

Lamb and Celery Casserole

Time required:
55 minutes

Servings: 02

INGREDIENTS	STEPS FOR COOKING
¼ cup celery stalk, chopped	1. Mix lamb chops with taco seasonings and put in the casserole mold.
2 lamb chops, chopped	2. Add celery stalk, coconut cream, and shredded mozzarella.
½ cup Mozzarella, shredded	3. Add butter, then cook the casserole in the preheated to 360F oven for 45 minutes.
1 teaspoon butter	
¼ cup coconut cream	
1 teaspoon taco seasonings	

Air Fried Salmon with Pesto

Time required:
17 minutes

Servings: 02

INGREDIENTS	STEPS FOR COOKING
¼ cup pesto ¼ cup sliced almonds, roughly chopped 2 salmon fillets 2 tablespoons unsalted butter, melted	1. In a small bowl, mix pesto and almonds. Set aside. 2. Place fillets into a 6 -inch round baking dish. 3. Brush each fillet with butter and place half of the pesto mixture on the top of each fillet, then place the dish into the air fryer basket. 4. Set the temperature to 390ºF and the timer for 12 minutes. 5. Salmon will easily flake when fully cooked and reach an internal temperature of at least 145ºF (63ºC). Serve warm.

Salmon Sushi Rolls

Time required:
25 minutes

Servings: 02

INGREDIENTS	STEPS FOR COOKING
4 sheets of roasted seaweed (nori) *100g smoked salmon* *100g full-fat cream cheese* *1 avocado* *½ cucumber* *2 tbsps soy sauce (optional)*	1. Place the sheet of roasted seaweed on a dry chopping board. With a sharp knife, cut each sheet of nori into 4 pieces. Repeat with the rest of the seaweed until you have 16 squares of nori. 2. Cut the cucumber into thin slices. Chop the avocado and smoked salmon into 16 pieces of a similar length to the cucumber, but thicker in width. 3. Fill a small bowl with water and set it down next to the chopping board. 4. Scoop a heaping teaspoon of cream cheese onto the nori sheet. Arrange lengthways with your fingers. 5. Add a piece of smoked salmon and avocado lengthways to the seaweed

INGREDIENTS	STEPS FOR COOKING
	sheet, followed by a couple of pieces of cucumber.
	6. Dip your fingertips into the bowl of water, then carefully seal up the sushi roll. The water should make it easier to close the seams.
	7. Repeat until all the sushi rolls have been made.
	8. Serve alone or with soy sauce.

Club Salad

Time required:
10 minutes

Servings: 02

INGREDIENTS	STEPS FOR COOKING

300g chopped Romaine lettuce

150g cucumber

110g cheddar or Edam cheese

15g cherry tomatoes

2 hard-boiled eggs

½ red onion

2 tbsp sour cream

1 tbsp mayonnaise

1 tsp heavy whipping cream

1. Dice the red onion, halve the cherry tomatoes, and quarter-slice the cucumber into bite-sized pieces.

2. Slice the hard-boiled eggs into wedges and cube your chosen cheese.

3. In a separate bowl, combine the mayonnaise, sour cream, and heavy whipping cream. Stir to fully combine and make a dressing.

4. Add lettuce to a serving bowl along with the onion, cucumber, tomatoes, and cheese cubes. Scoop the dressing onto the greens and mix well.

5. Top with the wedges of hard-boiled egg and serve.

Crispy Bacon Salad with Mozzarella and Tomato

Time required:
10 minutes

_____

Servings: 02

INGREDIENTS

1 large tomato, sliced

4 basil leaves

8 mozzarella cheese slices

2 teaspoons olive oil

6 bacon slices, chopped

1 teaspoon balsamic vinegar

Sea salt, to taste

STEPS FOR COOKING

1. Place the bacon in a skillet over medium heat and cook until crispy.

2. Divide the tomato slices between two plates.

3. Arrange the mozzarella slices over and top with the basil leaves.

4. Add the crispy bacon on top, drizzle with olive oil and vinegar.

5. Sprinkle with sea salt and serve.

Seared Scallops Topped with Wasabi Mayo

Time required:
20 minutes

Servings: 02

INGREDIENTS	STEPS FOR COOKING

1 tsp. wasabi paste

1 tsp. water

1 tbsp. butter

2 tbsp. mayonnaise

2 slices ginger, pickled, chopped

8 large sea scallops

Black pepper chives, chopped

Salt

1. Combine the wasabi paste and mayonnaise and mix well to incorporate. Use a paper towel to pat the scallops dry and season with salt and pepper.

2. In a skillet, heat the butter over medium-high heat. When the butter starts to brown, add the scallops and sear for about 1 ½ minute on each side. Place the scallops on two plates—4 scallops each—and add a dollop of wasabi mayo.

3. Finalize by topping with pickled ginger and fresh chives. Serve immediately.

Lemon Brussels Sprouts with Garlic

Time required:
35 minutes

Servings: 02

INGREDIENTS

2 cups of Brussels sprouts

3-5 cloves of garlic

1 tbsp avocado oil

Salt and Pepper to taste

STEPS FOR COOKING

1. Preheat oven to 400° F, then wash and dry the sprouts.
2. Cut in half and lose outer leaves. Place them on a baking sheet.
3. Cut the garlic cloves and cut them into large pieces.
4. Mix the sprouts and garlic with avocado oil, salt, and pepper. Bake for 15 min, then stir sprouts and garlic.
5. Cook another 15 to 20 min (the total cooking time depends on the size of your sprouts).

Parmesan Mackerel Fillet

Time required:
17 minutes

_____

Servings: 02

INGREDIENTS	STEPS FOR COOKING

12 ounces (340 g) mackerel fillet

2 ounces (57 g) Parmesan, grated

1 teaspoon ground coriander

1 tablespoon olive oil

1. Sprinkle the mackerel fillet with olive oil and put it in the air fryer basket.
2. Top the fish with ground coriander and Parmesan.
3. Cook the fish at 390ºF for 7 minutes.

Keto Hawaiian Pizza

Time required:
70 minutes

Servings: 02

INGREDIENTS	STEPS FOR COOKING

For the Pizza Crust:

280g cauliflower florets

100g grated parmesan cheese

1 large egg

½ tsp onion powder

½ tsp extra virgin olive oil

For the Pizza Topping:

120g shredded mozzarella cheese

100g tomato paste

75g sliced ham or Canadian bacon

60g finely diced pineapple

1. Preheat the oven to 200°C.

2. Begin by ricing the cauliflower florets. For the most ease, use a food processor. However, a box grater with small holes can also be used through this requires a bit more time and effort.

3. Heat a pan with no oil at medium-high heat. Cook the cauliflower until extremely soft, about 10 minutes. Stir frequently to ensure that all moisture is cooked off.

4. While the cauliflower is cooking, beat the egg in a large bowl. Once smooth, add the parmesan cheese and onion powder.

5. Remove the fried cauliflower from the pan once it looks soft and dry. Mix

INGREDIENTS	STEPS FOR COOKING

1 tsp basil

1 tsp oregano

1 tsp garlic powder

into the large bowl with the egg and cheese mixture until you have a dough. Make sure to fully combine, using a spatula if necessary.

6. Lightly grease some parchment paper with olive oil and transfer the cauliflower dough. Separate the dough into two balls, but if you have a tray that fits a large-sized pizza, feel free to keep it as one.

7. Flatten the dough with your hands to your desired thickness, but no less than 0.5cm and no more than 1cm. You may use a rolling pin for this step if you prefer. Lastly, raise the edges of the dough to form the pizza crust.

8. Bake for 20 minutes.

9. While the pizza crust bakes heat a pan over medium-low heat. Add the tomato paste and about 50-60ml of water.

10. Use your spatula to stir and fully blend the paste and water. Simmer for 3- 4 minutes or until the sauce looks slightly thickened.

11. Season with salt and pepper, then stir in the basil, oregano, and garlic powder.

12. Allow the un-topped pizza to cool for 3-5 minutes before adding your toppings.

13. Add a layer of tomato sauce to the pizza, followed by another layer of

INGREDIENTS	STEPS FOR COOKING
	mozzarella cheese. Top with bacon or ham and pineapple chunks.

14. Bake for 10 minutes.
15. Serve and enjoy.

Cheesy Bell Pepper Pizza

Time required:
60 minutes

Servings: 02

INGREDIENTS

6 oz. mozzarella,
grated

2 tablespoons cream
cheese

2 tablespoons
Parmesan cheese

1 teaspoon oregano

½ cup almond flour

2 tablespoons
psyllium husk

4 oz. grated cheddar
cheese

¼ cup marinara
sauce

2/3 Bell pepper,
sliced

1 tomato, sliced

STEPS FOR COOKING

1. Preheat the oven to 4000 F. Combine all crust ingredients in a bowl, except for the mozzarella. Melt mozzarella in a microwave.

2. Stir it into the bowl and mix to combine, then divide the dough into 2.

3. Roll out the crusts in circles and place them on a lined baking sheet. Bake for 10 minutes.

4. Top with cheddar, marinara, bell pepper, tomato, and basil. Replace it in the oven and bake for 10 minutes. Serve with olives.

INGREDIENTS

2 tablespoons chopped basil

6 black olives

STEPS FOR COOKING

Cucumber Shrimp Bites with Guacamole

Time required:
25 minutes

Servings: 02

INGREDIENTS	STEPS FOR COOKING

INGREDIENTS

100g large shrimp
(deveined and
peeled)

1 cucumber

1 avocado

½ lime

1 tbsp of extra virgin
olive oil

¼ tsp cayenne
pepper

¼ tsp garlic powder

STEPS FOR COOKING

1. Cut cucumber so there is one slice for every piece of shrimp.

2. In a bowl, coat shrimp in olive oil, onion powder, cayenne pepper, salt, and black pepper.

3. Cook shrimp over medium-high heat in your chosen oil. About 3 minutes on each side.

4. Mash the avocado in a bowl. Squeeze lime juice and season with salt. Combine into a blended mixture.

5. Spoon avocado mixture so it covers each cucumber slice. Top with shrimp pieces.

6. Serve with lime wedges as a garnish and enjoy.

Fried Soft-Shell Crab

Time required:
20 minutes

Servings: 02

INGREDIENTS	STEPS FOR COOKING

INGREDIENTS

4 tbsp. barbecue sauce

½ cup lard

½ cup parmesan cheese, powdered

2 eggs, beaten

8 soft shell crabs

STEPS FOR COOKING

1. Heat a skillet with lard over medium-high heat. Use a paper towel to pat the crabs dry. Prepare the parmesan and eggs by placing them in separate shallow dishes.

2. Dip one crab into the egg, tap off any excess, and dip into the parmesan cheese. Make sure the crab is coated well and evenly. Drop batches of crabs into the oil and cook for about 2 minutes on each side.

3. Serve the crabs hot with barbecue sauce for dipping.

Onion Rings

Time required:
30 minutes

Servings: 02

INGREDIENTS

1 medium onion, cut
into ½-inch thick
rings

½ cup coconut flour

1 tablespoon heavy
whipping cream

2 large organic eggs

½ cup Parmesan
cheese, grated

2 ounces pork rinds,
crushed

STEPS FOR COOKING

1. Preheat your oven to 425°F, then arrange a greased rack onto a large baking sheet.

2. Break apart the onion rings and discard inside pieces.

3. In a shallow bowl, place coconut flour.

4. In a second shallow bowl, add heavy cream and egg and beat until well combined.

5. In a third shallow bowl, mix together Parmesan cheese and pork rinds.

6. Coat onion rings with coconut flour, then dip into the egg mixture, and finally, coat with cheese mixture.

7. Repeat the procedure of coating once.

8. Arrange the coated onion rings onto a prepared rack in a single layer.

9. Bake for approximately 15 minutes.

10. Serve warm.

Fluffy Eggs

Time required:
25 minutes

Servings: 02

INGREDIENTS	STEPS FOR COOKING
2 bacon slices *2 egg whites* *1 teaspoon butter*	1. Put the bacon in the skillet. 2. Add butter and roast the bacon for 2 minutes per side. 3. Meanwhile, whisk the egg whites until fluffy. 4. Pour the egg whites over the bacon and close the lid. 5. Cook on low heat for 10 minutes.

Zucchini Noodles with Avocado Sauce

Time required:
10 minutes

Servings: 02

INGREDIENTS

1 zucchini

1 ¼ cup basil

⅓ cup water

4 pine nuts tbsp

2 tbsp lemon juice

1 avocado

12 sliced cherry tomatoes

STEPS FOR COOKING

1. Make zucchini noodles with a peeler or a spiralizer.
2. Mix remaining ingredients (except cherry tomatoes) in a blender until smooth.
3. Mix noodles, avocado sauce, and cherry tomatoes in a bowl.

Delicious Berry Crunch

Time required:
15 minutes

Servings: 02

INGREDIENTS

2 tbsp almond flour

1 tsp cinnamon

1/2 cup pecans, chopped

2 tbsp coconut oil

1/4 tsp Xanthan gum

1/4 cup Erythritol

1 tsp vanilla

20 blackberries

STEPS FOR COOKING

1. Add blackberries, vanilla, erythritol, and xanthan gum into the heat-safe dish. Stir well.

2. Mix almond flour, cinnamon, pecans, and coconut oil and sprinkle over blackberry mixture—then cover the dish with foil.

3. Pour 1 cup of water into the instant pot, then place the trivet in the pot.

4. Place dish on top of the trivet.

5. Seal pot with lid and cook on high for 4 minutes.

6. Once done, release pressure using quick release. Remove lid.

7. . Serve and enjoy.

Blackberries Chia Seed Pudding

Time required:
35 minutes

Servings: 02

INGREDIENTS	STEPS FOR COOKING

1 cup full-fat natural yogurt

2 tsp swerve

2 tbsp chia seeds

1 cup fresh blackberries

1 tbsp lemon zest

Mint leaves, to serve

1. Mix together the yogurt and the swerve. Stir in the chia seeds.
2. Reserve 4 blackberries for garnish and mash the remaining blackberries with a fork until pureed. Stir in the yogurt mixture
3. Chill in the fridge for 30 minutes.
4. When cooled, divide the mixture into 2 glasses.
5. Top each with a couple of raspberries and mint leaves and serve.

Coffee Mint Pie

Time required:
40 minutes

Servings: 02

INGREDIENTS	STEPS FOR COOKING

INGREDIENTS

1 tablespoon instant coffee

2 tablespoons almond butter, softened

2 tablespoons erythritol

1 teaspoon dried mint

3 eggs, beaten

1 teaspoon spearmint, dried

4 teaspoons coconut flour

Cooking spray

STEPS FOR COOKING

1. Spray the air fryer basket with cooking spray, then mix all ingredients in the mixer bowl.

2. When you get a smooth mixture, transfer it to the air fryer basket. Flatten it gently.

3. Cook the pie at 365F (185ºC) for 25 minutes.

Chocolate Lava Cake

Time required:
20 minutes

Servings: 02

INGREDIENTS	STEPS FOR COOKING
2 ounces 85% cocoa chocolate	1. Start to preheat oven to 350F. Grease two ramekins with ghee.
1 tbsp. almond flour	2. Melt 2 ounces ghee and chocolate in a saucepan on low heat. Stir to combine and set aside.
2 ounces ghee, plus more for greasing	
2 eggs	3. Whisk eggs, salt, and vanilla until frothy.
1 tsp. vanilla extract	
2 tbsp. powdered erythritol	4. Add egg mixture, the chocolate mixture, with sweetener and almond flour, then mix to combine.
1 tbsp. granulated erythritol	
1/8 tsp. sea salt	5. Fill two ramekins halfway with the batter.
2 tbsp. 85% chocolate chunks	6. Add chocolate chunks and add the remaining batter, then bake until tops are set but still jiggly, about 9 minutes.
Fresh raspberries, almond butter for garnish	
	7. Cool, garnish, and serve.

Lime and Vanilla Cheesecake

Time required:
25 minutes

Servings: 02

INGREDIENTS	STEPS FOR COOKING

1/4 cup cream cheese, softened

2 tbsp heavy cream

1 tsp lime juice

1 egg

1 tsp pure vanilla extract

2-4 tbsp Erythritol or Stevia

1. In a microwave-safe bowl combine all ingredients, then place in a microwave and cook on HIGH for 90 seconds.
2. Every 30 seconds stir to combine the ingredients well.
3. Transfer mixture to a bowl, then refrigerate for at least 2 hours.
4. Before serving top with whipped cream or coconut powder.

Instant Coffee Ice Cream

Time required:
20 minutes

Servings: 02

INGREDIENTS	STEPS FOR COOKING

INGREDIENTS

1 tbsp Instant Coffee

2 tbsp Cocoa Powder

1 cup coconut milk

1/4 cup heavy cream

1/4 tsp flax seeds

2 tbsp Erythritol

15 drops liquid Nutria

STEPS FOR COOKING

1. Add all ingredients except the flax seeds into a container of your immersion blender.

2. Blend well until all ingredients are incorporated well. Slowly add in flax seeds until a slightly thicker mixture is formed. Add the mass to your ice cream machine and follow the manufacturer's instructions.

3. Ready! Serve!

Blueberry, Dates, and Banana Cream

Time required:
5 minutes

Servings: 02

INGREDIENTS	STEPS FOR COOKING
¾ cup blueberries 1 tablespoon peanut butter ¾ cup almond milk ½ banana, peeled 2 dates	1. In a blender, combine the blueberries with the milk, banana, butter, and dates, then pulse well. 2. Divide into 2 glasses and serve. 3. Enjoy!

Simple Icy Berry Popsicles

Time required:
5 minutes

Servings: 02

INGREDIENTS	STEPS FOR COOKING
2 c coconut cream *2 tsp of stevia* *¼ c of mixed blackberries and blueberries*	1. Blend the listed ingredients in a blender until smooth 2. Pour mix into popsicle molds and let them chill for 2 hours 3. Serve and enjoy!

Cinnamon Roll Chaffles

Time required:
10 minutes

Servings: 02

INGREDIENTS

1 tbsp. almond flour

1 tsp. cinnamon powder

1/2 cup cheddar cheese

1 tbsp. cocoa powder

½ tsp baking powder

1 large egg.

2 tbsps. peanut oil for topping

STEPS FOR COOKING

1. Preheat the waffle maker and mix together all ingredients in a bowl. Pour the chaffle mixture into the center of the greased waffle maker. Close the waffle maker.

2. Cook chaffles for about 4-5 minutes until cooked and crispy. Once chaffles are cooked, remove them.

3. Pour melted butter oil on top. Servings and enjoy!

Vanilla Chocolate Chips Soufflés

Time required:
20 minutes

Servings: 02

INGREDIENTS	STEPS FOR COOKING

2 large eggs, whites, and yolks separated

1 teaspoon vanilla extract

2 ounces (57 g) low-carb chocolate chips

2 teaspoons coconut oil, melted

1. In a medium bowl, beat egg whites until stiff peaks form, about 2 minutes. Set aside.

2. In another medium bowl, whisk egg yolks and vanilla together. Set aside.

3. In a microwave-safe bowl, place chocolate chips and drizzle with coconut oil. Microwave on high for 20 seconds, then stir and continue cooking in 10-second increments until melted, being careful not to overheat the chocolate. Let cool for 1 minute.

4. Slowly pour melted chocolate into egg yolks, then whisk until smooth.

5. Begin adding egg white mixture to chocolate mixture, about ¼ cup at a time, folding in gently.

INGREDIENTS	STEPS FOR COOKING
	6. Pour mixture into two 4-inch ramekins greased with cooking spray. Place ramekins into air fryer basket.
	7. Adjust the temperature to 400°F (205ºC) and set the timer for 15 minutes, then soufflés will puff up while cooking and deflate a little once cooled. The center will be set when done. Let cool for 10 minutes.
	8. Serve warm.